G000269082

AMERICAN TRAVELER

CALIFORNIA

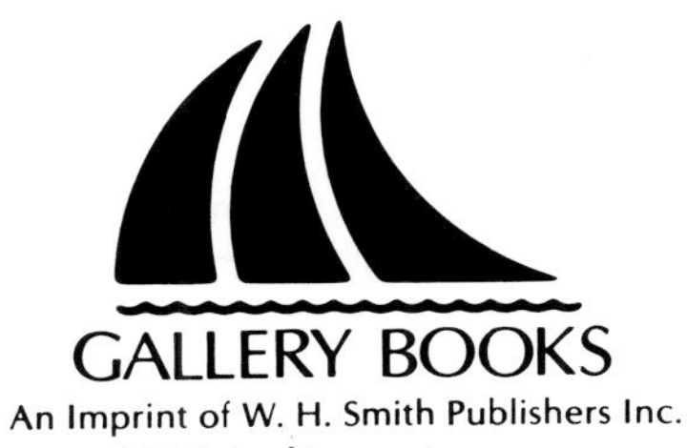

GALLERY BOOKS
An Imprint of W. H. Smith Publishers Inc.
112 Madison Avenue
New York City 10016

This edition first published in U.S.
in 1990 by Gallery Books,
an imprint of W.H. Smith Publishers, Inc.
112 Madison Avenue, New York, New York 10016

ISBN 0-8317-8828-3

Printed and bound in Spain

For rights information about the photographs in
this book please contact:

The Image Bank
111 Fifth Avenue, New York, N.Y. 10003

Producer: Solomon M. Skolnick
Author: Nancy Millichap Davies
Design Concept: Lesley Ehlers
Designer: Ann-Louise Lipman
Editor: Terri L. Hardin
Production: Valerie Zars
Photo Researcher: Edward Douglas
Assistant Photo Researcher: Robert Hale

Title page: *Twisted by coastal winds, a solitary cypress clings to its rocky perch along the coast south of Monterey.* Opposite: *A graceful grove of coast redwoods. California's state tree can grow to more than 200 feet in height, 25 feet in diameter.*

For nearly a century and a half, the name "California" has conjured up images of the fortunate paradise on the farther shore, a nearly mythical golden land at the end of the road west. The state's motto reflects this view of California as the place of promise: "Eureka," or "I have found it." Millions of Americans have headed westward to search for their gold at rainbow's end in California, with the result that the state is currently the nation's most populous, home to one U.S. resident in 10. Immigrants too flock to California, especially from eastern Asia and from Mexico. Overall, the population of the state grows by more than half a million annually.

Yet this California, a magnet to so many, is a different place for every resident, every visitor. It boasts not only unspoiled natural areas that remain much as they were known to the first Californians before the

This page: *Surf whitens offshore rocks in Salt Point State Park, a popular spot for whale-watching on the northern Sonoma coast. Near-horizontal beams of sunset light cast a red-gold glow across rough water along a rocky stretch of the northern coast. Monterey pines, natives of the Monterey Peninsula coast, screen the Pacific sunset as they lean away from the prevailing winds.* Opposite: *Since the 1860's, vineyards like this one in the narrow, fertile Napa Valley have been producing California wines.*

oming of Europeans, but also ophisticated cities which look the twenty-first century. It roduces tonight's television hows, tomorrow's dinner ine, and next year's compu- er. Each city, each region, ven each town within this iverse state has its own istinctive quality, often quite ndependent of the characters f its neighboring regions and rban areas.

That this should be the ase is hardly surprising. California is after all the hird-largest state in the U.S. n area. The state's terrain is ot only vast in expanse but mmensely varied in kind, vith areas as unlike one nother as the broad sun- renched beaches of the south, he cool, damp coastal forests f the north, and interior eserts of sand and stone. The tallest mountain in the ontinental U.S., 14,494-foot Mount Whitney, and the low- est spot in North America, Death Valley's Badwater at 282 feet below sea level, are oth within the state.

Opposite: *Sky-blue on the vine at harvest time, these cabernet sauvignon grapes will yield a wine redder than the leaf in the foreground.* This page: *All roads lead to wineries in Sonoma County's Dry Creek Valley. Vineyards from small "boutiques" to industry giants offer tours and tastings.* Right: *Sonoma barrels. California's wine industry began in this county in the mid-1800's with 100,000 vines that Hungarian Count Haraszthy imported from Europe.*

Patchy sunlight breaking through thick San Francisco Bay fog dapple a tower of the Golden Gate Bridge and its cables. Below: *Wind churns Pacific breakers and scours the sandy slopes of Point Reyes Nation Seashore, 30 miles north of San Francisco.* Opposite: *San Francisco symbol since its 1937 completion, th Golden Gate Bridge carries six lane of traffic to mile-distant Marin County.*

Spires atop Sts. Peter and Paul Roman Catholic Church, spiritual center of San Francisco's Italian district, command a bayside panorama. Below: *The lagoon before the Palace of Fine Arts, sole surviving building of the Panama-Pacific International Exposition of 1915, reflects its rotunda and colonnades.*

Turn-of-the-century San Francisco town houses on Steiner Street pose a sharp contrast of shape and scale with the downtown skyline beyond. Below: *Colorful signs in two alphabets cluster above the streets of San Francisco's Chinatown, reputedly the largest Chinese settlement outside the Orient.*

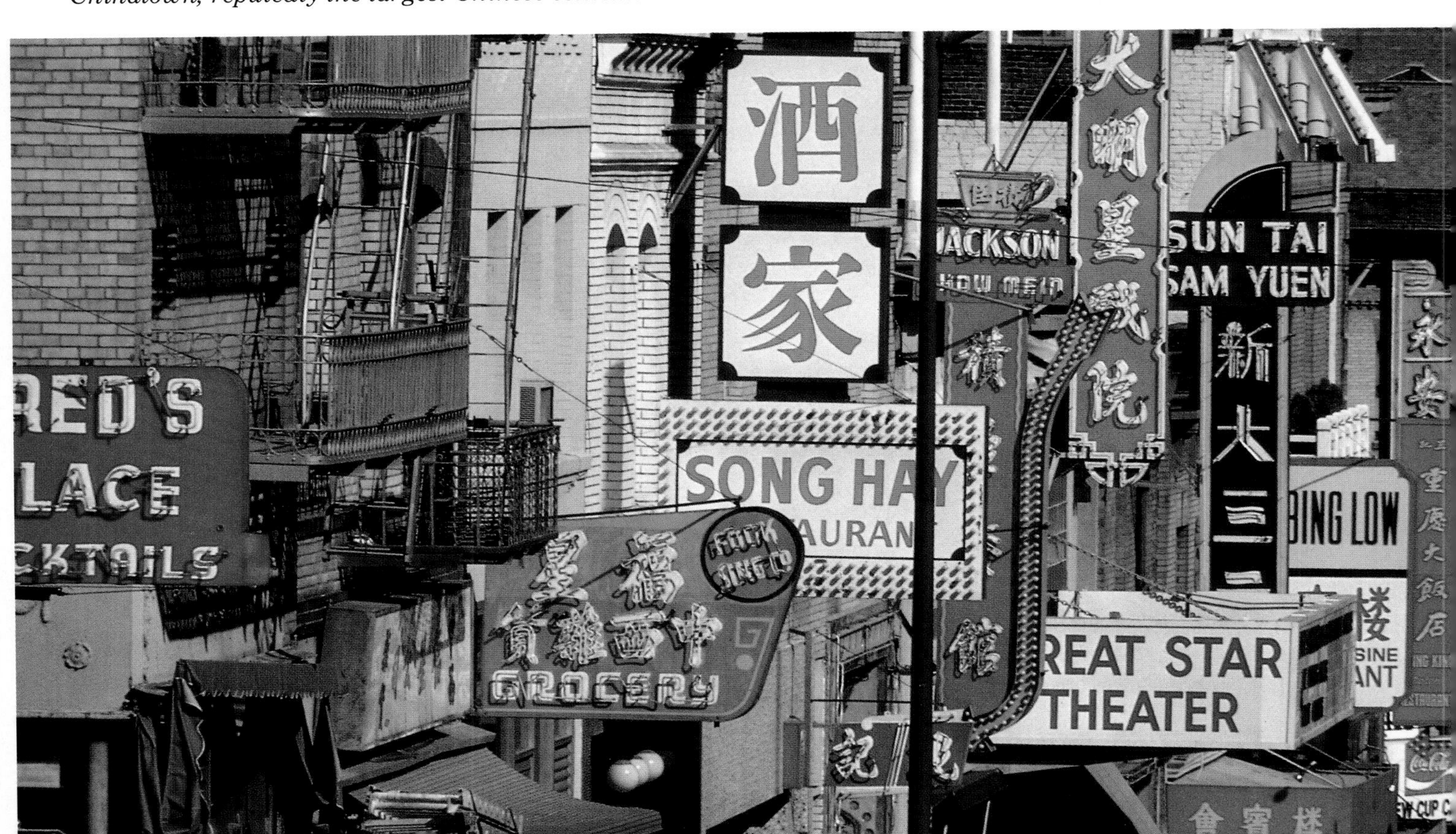

POWELL AND MARKET
AQUATIC PARK
MARITIME MUSEUM
HYDE AND BEACH
FISHERMAN'S WHARF
4 BLOCKS FROM TERMINAL
20
"I stop at the St. Francis"

California has its living
ıperlatives as well. In
equoia National Park, the
iant sequoia known as the
eneral Sherman Tree stands
75 feet tall and measures
6 feet around its base, the
ırgest living thing in the
orld. The world's oldest
ving things are the bristle-
one pines growing high in
ıe White Mountains of the
ierra Nevada, one of which
s known to be at least
,600-years-old.

The state's entries in the
ecord books also include a
,200-mile-long coast, one-
enth of the total U.S. shore-
ıne. Scattered as they are
long the Pacific in a large,
ong, and relatively narrow
tate, Californians find it
ıatural to speak in terms of
ıorthern versus southern
California. In the public
nind, these two distinct
egions are closely identified
vith their respective great
ities, San Francisco and Los
Angeles, and contrasts be-
ween the two are pronounced.

)pposite: *A cable car of the Powell-Hyde line heads toward Fisherman's Wharf. Nostalgia and city vistas are ımong the attractions of the journey.* This page: *San Francisco's Financial District skyline as seen from Nob Hill. The arresting shape of the Transamerica Pyramid is ınmistakable at left. Fisherman's Wharf at dusk. Behind wharves where the fleet is anchored for the ıight, waterside restaurants light up o offer shore dinners. The glittering owers of the Embarcadero Center lwarf the 1898 Ferry Building with ts clock tower, San Francisco andmark of an earlier era.*

Preceding page: *On its way to Oakland, the graceful span of the Bay Bridge arcs above a sparkling vista of the San Francisco waterfront.* This page: *The Winchester "Mystery" House, San Jose. Built b a widowed heiress who believed sh would die if it the house were completed, it contains 160 rooms. The last orchard in Silicon Valley. Much of Santa Clara County's rich farmland has fallen prey to the dramatic expansion of technologica industry.* Opposite: *The eroding powers of waves and winds combined to carve out this rock arc at Natural Bridges State Beach, Santa Cruz.* Below: *A Monterey cypress stands guard on Midway Point on the Seventeen Mile Drive i Pebble Beach; visitors admire the spectacular view.*

Stillness reigns on the Monterey waterfront, a commercial fishing center when John Steinbeck made it the setting of his 1945 novel Cannery Row.

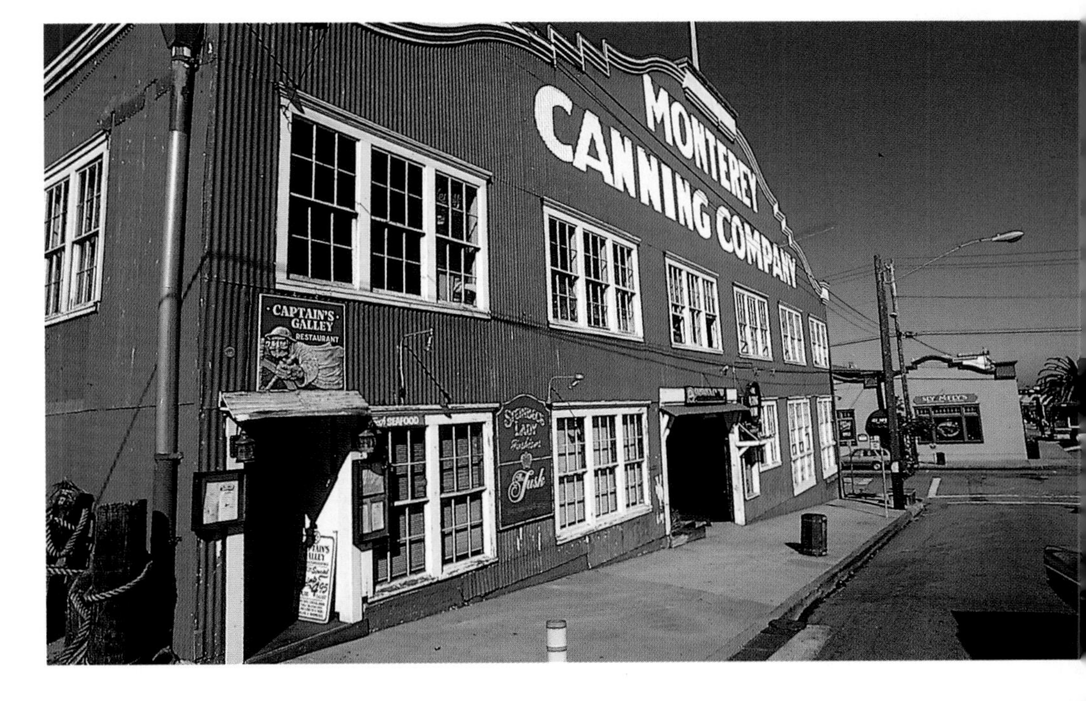

ɔp to bottom: *The central fountain ıd bell tower of the Presidio Chapel 'San Carlos Borromeo in Monterey, unded in 1770. Once a street of 30 ırdine canneries, Ocean View venue in Monterey is now the site 'restaurants and shops. John teinbeck, the 1962 Nobel laureate literature, was born in 1902 in is Salinas house; it is now a onprofit restaurant.*

San Francisco, long known s "the City" because it was ıe first and for decades the nly significant metropolitan rea in the state, clusters ɔmpactly on 46 square miles f a peninsula thrusting up ıumblike between the acific and San Francisco ay. Los Angeles, an incor-oration of many small ıdependent communities 'hose boundaries became lurred as development roceeded in the first half of ıis century, sprawls over 465 quare miles.

Nostalgic San Franciscans pare no effort to maintain he relatively few buildings hat survived its 1906 earth-uake and fire, and they have lmost as much affection for hose built shortly afterward. 'he phoenix, a mythical bird eborn from its own ashes, s the city's emblem. San 'rancisco also keeps cable ars clanging up its hills at ess than 10 miles an hour not ecause they are efficient but ecause they are charming. It s a city very much aware of ts past.

The village of Carmel, an artists' colony popular with weekend travelers for its quaint houses and splendid setting above the white beaches of Carmel Bay. Below: *Pebble Beach, an elegant residential area on Seventeen Mile Drive below Monterey. Golfers gather on this course for the annual AT&T National Pro-Am tournament.* Opposite: *Inland from Monterey in the Galiban Range, the rock spires of Pinnacles National Monument twist up to heights of a thousand feet.*

Angelenos, on the other hand, hold in particular regard their many examples of up-to-the-minute contemporary design, including the gleaming skyscrapers of a downtown that since the Second World War has been transformed by urban renewa The mood of Los Angeles is perhaps best suggested by th onrushing movement of its freeways: a city giving the rear-view mirror only an occasional glance, cruising along in the fast lane toward tomorrow.

California's population is heavily concentrated in four areas: San Francisco, Los Angeles, the San Diego area, and the rich agricultural region of the Central Valley around Sacramento, the capital. By comparison, the state's generally arid eastern sector is sparsely settled. The most unforgettable scenery lies in the many extensive natural areas where development has left few traces or none.

Much of this wild beauty depends on the contrasts of elevation provided by the mountains which encircle California. Down that extensive sweep of Pacific shore run the coastal ranges often fronted, as at Big Sur, by steep cliffs plunging down to the sea before them. Beyond the long, fertile strip of the Central Valley, the vast high region that the Spanish calle Sierra Nevada, "snowy mountains," lies along the

Preceding page: *Forming a series o capes, the cliffs of rocky headlands on the Big Sur coast plunge towar the sea and its drifting fog.* This page: *In 1889, Big Sur ranchers anchored this lighthouse high abou the rough water at the base of the immense promontory known as Point Sur.* Below: *Passengers in ca crossing Big Sur's Bixby Creek Bridge on California State Route 1 enjoy sweeping views of canyon an coast.* Opposite: *On Big Sur's Pfeiffer Beach, sunlight spangles th surf as it crashes through a blowho into a sea cave.*

state's eastern border. Its wild, frigid peaks and its groves of giant sequoias are sheltered from the threat of extensive commercial development within three nationa parks and eight national forests. To the north, the rugged Cascades dip in from Oregon; Mount Shasta and the active volcano of Lassen Peak are among the most notable.

Millions of Californians spend their leisure time outdoors in the extensive wilderness, on the glorious beaches, or at home on patios in pools, in hot tubs. A climate which, in most settled areas, offers an agreeable combination of mild or even subtropical temperatures and long periods of uninterrupted sunshine has, not surprisingly bred a population of nature lovers. One natural force widely evident in the state, however, remains the subject of fascination and terror: earthquakes.

This page: *An extravagant blend of European styles distinguishes San Simeon, the hilltop "ranch" designe by architect Julia Morgan for newspaper magnate William Randolph Hearst. At the Hearst estate at San Simeon, a classical temple to Neptune stands beside the white marble pool, which holds 250,000 gallons of water. San Simeon's hundred-foot-long Roman Pool, surrounded by classical sculptures from the vast collection Hearst imported from the Old Worl* Opposite: *Inspired by Spanish renaissance design, cathedral-like bell towers dominate the façade of the main house at San Simeon.*

Santa Ines Mission
FOUNDED
MASSES
Sundays-8-9:30-11 am
12:30 pm.
Daily-8 am.
NO PARKING ANY TIME

Opposite: *The restored bell tower at the main entrance of the 1817 Santa Inés Mission outside Solvang.* This page: *Buildings and a street sign with Scandinavian style hint at the heritage of Solvang, founded by Danes from the Midwest in 1911.* Below: *Mandysland Farm in the Santa Ynez Valley. Irrigated fields, green and smooth, contrast sharply with the dry surrounding hillsides.*

This page: *Alongside Santa Barbara's 84-acre harbor for pleasure craft, flags flap above the half-mile-long breakwater which protects the municipal beach.* Below: *Off to catch a wave, a surfer heading north of Malibu Pier and the board he carries become silhouettes in the late-day sun.* Opposite: *The Santa Barbara Mission, with its square front towers and classical façade, may be the best-preserved of the 21 original missions.*

Palms on neighboring hilltops bracket a view of the far-flung expanse of Los Angeles alight beneath a rose-and-purple sunset.

ɒp to bottom: The 260-acre Century ty high-rise complex in West Los ngeles, erected in the 1960's on the rmer site of the Twentieth-Century ɒx studio. Car lights streaking this me-lapse photograph suggest the aseless traffic on the Harbor reeway in downtown Los Angeles. t the Music Center for the rforming Arts in Los Angeles, the ark Taper Forum and the Pavilion ckon lovers of concerts and drama.

The state's scenic moun-in regions are lined with aults," lines of weakness in e earth's very crust. The mous San Andreas fault, hich runs from Mendocino ounty 650 miles south along e Coast Range, was the picenter of the 1989 earth-uake. It is only the best-nown of hundreds of fault nes, all likely epicenters.

Many of the state's oldest uildings, including the panish missions, have suf-red at least some earth-uake damage. The most mous quake, and arguably e most devastating in terms property damage and loss of fe, was the one that struck an Francisco in 1906. It robably measured 8.3 on the ichter scale, a system of auging earthquake severity vented afterward. While the amage caused by the two-inute quake was extensive, r more property destruction sulted from the fires that llowed, disastrous in a city here more than 85 percent the structures were made of

This page: *The City Hall, with its 464-foot tower, was Los Angeles' tallest building when it was completed in 1928; recent sky-scrapers reach over twice that height. Exterior elevators climb between the mirror-faced cylindric towers of the Los Angeles Westin Bonaventure Hotel, offering expansive city views.* Opposite: *Monoliths of the 1970's, the sleek glass exteriors of corporate high-rises reflect the sun–as well as eac other–in downtown Los Angeles.*

wood. Three-quarters of the houses in the city were destroyed. The 1989 quake, which measured 7.1 on the Richter scale and interrupte the World Series, was far les destructive overall, mostly because strict building codes in today's San Francisco require that all new construc tion be able to withstand major tremors.

Alarming as they are, earthquakes are nothing nev on the California scene. Geologic evidence suggests that they have been rearran ing the Californian landscap for many millions of years. The record of life forms in California began late, yet long before humans came to the area. Perhaps the most celebrated prehistoric site in the state is the La Brea Pits, oozing oily bogs near Los Angeles which entrapped millions of birds and animal during the Pleistocene and I Ages. Since 1906, skeletons sabre-tooth tigers, woolly

mammoths, giant ground sloths, and other long-extinct species have been recovered at the site.

The first human settlements came much later, as Native American populations grew in the fertile valleys. European colonists discovered and named the region in the early 1500's. The Spanish writer Montalvo had coined the name "California" for a mythical earthly paradise in his 1510 romance "Las Serges de Esplandian," and some anonymous Spanish conquistador gave the name in turn to the newly discovered area of what is today northwest Mexico as well as what is now southern California.

The Los Angeles Farmer's Market in Hollywood offers lavish displays of fresh produce, a variety of shops, and outdoor dining. Below: *Replicas of imperial elephants at the La Brea Pits, bogs of underground oil and tar that have yielded finds of Ice Age animals.* Opposite: *Italian-born folk artist Simon Rodia created these filligree steel towers in Watts, Los Angeles, between 1921 and 1954.*

This page: Neon-bright against the night sky, the Oriental fantasy of a movie palace known as the Chinese Theater has been a Hollywood landmark since 1927. Left: *Concrete handprints and footprints of movie stars decorate the Chinese Theater's entry court. Some bear dedications to the theater's founder, Sidney Grauman.* Opposite top to bottom: *The sheet-metal letters of the Hollywood sign, 50 feet tall and 30 feet wide, advertised a housing development when erected in 1929. The secluded luxury of the Beverly Hills Hotel, built in 1919, typifies the style of the residential area near Hollywood which many movie stars call home. Intersection of Hollywood and Vine Streets, center of the downtown business district and onetime heart of the entertainment industry.*

The state's early history
ıakes it especially fitting
ıat California should be
ome today to the largest
Iispanic population in the
Inited States. Its first
uropean settlers came from
pain, and Spanish colonists–
oth soldiers and those in
oly orders–shaped the
egion's cultural traditions.
'hey left a legacy of places
hose names begin with the
panish designations for male
nd female saints. Among
'alifornia's dozens of "Sans"
nd "Santas" are the 21
ıission settlements which
panish Franciscan priests
ɔunded in the late 1700's,
ıostly along the coast. At
rst outposts of religious and
gricultural control by the
panish (later the Mexican)
uthorities, many of the
ıissions later became centers
f transportation and settle-
ıent. San Francisco was
ɔunded as the sixth of the
ıissions, "San Francisco de
sís," or Saint Francis of
ssisi. Los Angeles–"Pueblo
e Nuestra Señora la Reina
e Los Angeles de Porciúncula,"
r Town of Our Lady the
Queen of the Angels of
'orciúncula–was also
ɔunded in the early days,
ut as a colonial town near
Iission San Gabriel, not as a
ıission itself. San Francisco
he high-minded, Los Angeles
he worldly: some would
rgue that the distinction
olds to this day.

Sailboats dot the bay beyond the Carousel Building on Santa Monica Pier. The restored 1916 structure houses an antique carousel with 44 hand-carved horses. Below: *As visitors stare, both sexes pump iron on the Beachwalk in Venice. Gold's Gym in the background is a mecca for bodybuilders.*

By the middle of the nineteenth century, California's ongoing story was being written in a new language. English had replaced Spanish, and Washington, D.C. had replaced Mexico as the distant source of authority. California was admitted to the Union as a free state in 1850. In the same period, the link between California and gold was formed in the public mind when news of the strike at Sutter's Mill on American Creek north of San Francisco reached the East Coast, drawing prospectors from around the nation and, eventually, the world. The population of the state, 15,000 at the time of the strike, multiplied to 25 times that number within 12 years. Many who came seeking their fortunes remained to settle, including the Chinese laborers who had been encouraged to emigrate to California to perform the hard physical labor of gold-mining. Soon they, and others who had not struck gold and needed work, were building California's all important overland link to the east: the railroad.

After the tracks of the Union Pacific and the Central Pacific met at Promontory Point, Utah, in 1859, California was no longer a remote destination accessible only by a long sea journey. Rail company competition dropped ticket prices to affordable levels, luring settlers from the east who yearned for fertile farmland and a mild, sunny limate. The great migration vest that began with the Gold Rush has continued ever ince.

The reports of good land vere true. Even in this high-ech era, farming continues to e the most productive indus-ry in the state. The Central Valley, which runs from Sacramento to San Joaquin, as been called the world's nost fertile growing region. t contains two-thirds of the tate's farmland. Farmers and anchers also operate in the oastal valleys and in the

Pleasure craft crowd the harbor of Avalon Bay on Santa Catalina Island, a 27-mile sail from Los Angeles harbor. The Santa Monica Mountains form a dramatic backdrop for the city's waterfront hotels. Here, lights on the beach shine through evening mist.

This page, right: *In Anaheim's Disneyland, always a place for the unexpected, a half-moon shines by day above the Sleeping Beauty Castle.* Below: *Two Disneyland fantasies.* Background: *The Mark Twain Steamboat ride in Frontierland.* Foreground: *Masts of the Columbia Sailing Ship.* Opposite: *Mission San Juan Capistrano, ca. 1797, considered California's oldest building. Its great church collapsed in an 1812 quake; swallow-haunted ruins remain.* Overleaf: *San Diego by night. The city, seventh-largest in the U.S., owes its growth to its great natural harbors.*

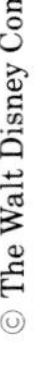

'pposite: *Bands of fluted rock, ıbtle color variations, and the play f hillside shadows add depth to this ındscape in Anza-Borrego Desert tate Park.* This page: *Flowers of the edgehog cactus provide brilliant ontrast with the grays and greens of rock-crowned desert hillside at the oshua Tree National Monument.* *elow: The chic desert resort of 'alm Springs, noted for its greeable climate and its golf ourses. Celebrities have wintered ere since the 1930's.*

irrigated Imperial Valley in the southeast. The climate and topography of the state are so varied that virtually every temperate-climate and subtropical crop can be raised somewhere. A large percentage of the fresh fruit and vegetables consumed elsewhere in the nation comes from California, which also produces 85 percent of the U.S. output of wine. And illegal though it remains, marijuana is estimated to be one of the most profitable crops in the state where the Beats of the 1950's and the hippies of the 1960's first came to national attention.

In our own time, many Californians have become increasingly worried about the sacrifice of farmland to development, not only of malls in the home state of the shopping center but also of housing for a mushrooming population. By one estimate, each increase of 10 people in the state's population means that one acre of land is converted to non-agricultural use. Santa Clara County plums once provided a third of

Top to bottom: *On highway 190, an entrance sign for one of the world's hottest and driest places. Death Valley became a national monument in 1933. Ridges pattern the crystallized surface of salt flats stretching across the Death Valley floor. Summer temperatures here can reach 130° F. After heavy spring rains, yellow poppies spring up beneath the Joshua trees to carpet this valley floor in the Mojave Desert.*

ıe world's prunes; many ırmer orchards have disppeared beneath the parking ts of Silicon Valley, cradle of ıe microchip. The orange roves that gave Orange ounty its name, too, are fast eing replaced by new sub-.visions. The spread of cities ke Anaheim, where Disney-.nd is located, have made the ounty the second most heavy populated in the state, ırpassed only by neighborg Los Angeles County.

elow: *The tints of Death Valley's ricolored rocks vary hourly with e changing light.* Above: *Death alley sand dunes, sculpted by ind. Behind them rise the rugged ountains which form the walls of e narrow, 140-mile-long valley.*

A remarkable prospect is a view up the trunk of a giant sequoia. The tree may attain a 250-foot height and a diameter of 25 feet. Below: *The drive through this tunnel, a fallen sequoia in Sequoia National Park, gives visitors a clear sense of the rare tree's vast size.* Opposite: *A grove of giant sequoia trees, the largest living things on earth. Most now alive are found in California parklands.*

This page: *The California State Capitol, topped with a golden dome 237 feet high, stands in a 40-acre park in the center of Sacramento.* Below: *Wind-whipped snows crown Mount Whitney in Sequoia National Park, at 14,495 feet the highest U.S. peak outside Alaska.* Opposite: *The cones of two long-ago volcanoes top Mount Shasta, foremost peak in the California Cascades. Glaciers are found near its summit.* Below: *Evening descends on Lassen Peak, one of the few volcanoes in the continental U.S. now considered live. It was active from 1914 to 1921.*

Another important California enterprise, one that has transmitted the state's name and influence around the world, is the motion picture industry. Although the earliest U.S. film producers operated in New York, the first Los Angeles studio was established in 1906 and its first film made that year on a ranch in the area which would become Hollywood. Soon East Coast producers were heading west for locations which offered dependable sunshine, low rents, and a business climate favorable to small companies and stars were being born under the California sun. In the early years, each star was contracted exclusively to one

Among the summits of the Sierra Nevada, sunlit snow frosts rugged mountaintops and high-altitude lakes seem even bluer than the big sky. Below: *Climatic conditions on high Sierra slopes above this treeline become so severe that even hardy conifers like the lodgepole pine cannot survive.*

of a small circle of important production companies which dominated the industry: Fox, Metro, RKO, Warner Brothers. To show their movies, the studios also controlled chains of theaters around the country.

Most studios opened in Hollywood, which in 1911 ha been a small and conservativ residential town of 4,000 people. By the 1920's it was the home of a billion-dollar business, and the name "Hollywood" was synonymou with the glamorous and sometimes scandalous way of life of the directors, producer and stars. Movie celebrities built fabulous houses in Hollywood and in neighborin Beverly Hills. Sid Grauman staged gala premières at his extravagant movie palaces, the Egyptian Theater and th pseudo-Oriental Chinese Theater.

Before the Second World War, location filming was often confined to the studio and nearby environs. After that many directors began shooting elsewhere to save money. Also, when television gained popularity, it changed the movie industry dramati-

Opposite: *Like a ship at anchor, an uninhabited island stands out against the shining blue mirror of three-mile-long Emerald Bay, a cov of Lake Tahoe. Below: Pine branche honed by mountain weather point skyward before a snow-covered backdrop in the White Mountains o Inyo National Forest.*

ally. Hollywood moved with he times, eventually transorming itself into a center of elevision as well as feature ilm production. It continues o play both roles today, but roduction facilities have for lecades been located in the utlying regions of the town. The famous intersection of

)pposite: *Beyond the yellow flowers f rabbitbrush, tufa towers, formed y the meeting of underwater prings and salt water, rise on Mono ake's shore.* This page: *Once under vater, the weird shapes of tufa owers emerged as Mono Lake's level lropped.* Right: *Reflected in Mono Lake's still water, these limestone ufa shapes against the fantastic olors of a sunset sky suggest an nchanted castle.*

This page: *Devil's Postpile Nationa Monument in Inyo National Fores is made up of columns of solidified lava, formed underground and exposed by erosion.* Below: *Tumbli from a hanging valley left high wh glaciers gouged Yosemite Valley, misty Bridalveil Fall drops 620 fee* Opposite: *The south face of mighty Half Dome stands out beyond snou covered trees along the Merced Riv in Yosemite National Park.*

Hollywood and Vine at the center of Hollywood retains little of its onetime allure.

California, then, is a complex collection of elemen continually changing an interaction of a place abundant in earth's wonders and terrors and the humans who gave it a name and a history. Both the people of the state and those many visitors who come to do business, to marv at the fabled folkways of the land of the mellow, or merely to satisfy their curiosity cannot help but encounter an urban lifestyle that some say is always 10 years ahead of the rest of the country. Whatever their responses to the ongoing development of sprawling cities and suburbs, they are seldom disappointed in the splendor of the beaches mountains, and extensive wild lands. Those who gaze u at a snowy Sierra peak or down at the pounding waves of Big Sur might well believe in the exhilaration of the moment, that the promise of paradise on the farther shore has indeed been fulfilled. "Eureka," they might say.

This page: *Naturalist John Muir called Half Dome "the most beautiful and most sublime of all the wonderful Yosemite rocks."* Below: *In the Yosemite dawn, dark outlines of conifers and of Half Dome's granite top jut above a dense white blanket of fog.* Opposite: *Yosemite's Merced River reflects the sheer face of El Capitan. At 4,000 feet in height, it is the largest exposed monolith of granite in the world.* Overleaf: *Vast granite formations drop to forested valleys to form this Yosemite landscape, legacy of glacial action during several ice ages.*

Index of Photography

All photographs courtesy of The Image Bank, except where indicated.*